TUDOR TALES

Contents

Illustrations by

Lesley Danson

Mike Spoor

Andrew Oliver

A QUIET FAMILY CHRISTMAS

by Steve Barlow and Steve Skidmore

THE FAMILY OF KING HENRY VIII

First Wife
CATHERINE OF ARAGON
(married 1509, divorced 1533)
Daughter – **Mary**

Second Wife
ANNE BOLEYN
(married 1533, beheaded 1536)
Daughter – **Elizabeth**

Third Wife
JANE SEYMOUR
(married 1536, died 1537)
Son – **Edward**

Fourth Wife
ANNE OF CLEVES
(married 1540, divorced 1540)

Fifth Wife
CATHERINE HOWARD
(married 1540, beheaded 1542)

By December of 1542, Henry wanted to marry again.

Mary
King Henry's daughter, aged 26. Henry divorced her mother so he could marry Anne Boleyn. Very religious.

Elizabeth
Henry's daughter, aged nine. Her mother, Anne Boleyn, was beheaded. Cheerful and chatty, but stubborn.

Edward
Henry's son, aged five. His mother died when he was born. He is spoilt.

Will Sommers
King Henry's jester.

Catherine Parr
Catherine is 31.
She looks after Mary and Elizabeth. She is kind and sensible.

Thomas Seymour
A lord who wants to marry Catherine Parr.

Hampton Court Palace, Christmas Eve, 1542.

*A candlelit room. Catherine Parr and Thomas Seymour enter.
Thomas is carrying some Christmas presents.*

Thomas Catherine, when are we going to get married?

Catherine Look out, Thomas, you're dropping the presents.

Thomas drops some of the presents. Catherine picks them up and puts them back in his arms.

Thomas Spring – how about spring? *(Sings)* "In springtime ..."

Catherine Stand still.

Thomas Or why don't we get married this Christmas?

Catherine I don't think the King would like that.

Thomas He wouldn't mind. We could have a feast – he'd like that! We could invite all our friends.

Catherine Thomas, there's something I have to tell you.

Elizabeth runs in. Edward comes in behind her. He has a blindfold on. They are playing blind man's buff. He bumps into Thomas and makes him drop the presents.

Thomas Look out! Edward!

Edward grabs hold of Thomas.

Edward Who's this? It can't be Daddy – you're too thin. I know! You're Maggie the maid!

Elizabeth Wrong! You're wrong! It's Uncle Thomas.

Edward takes the blindfold off.

Edward Well, Lizzie, you try to do it.

Elizabeth I don't have to. You didn't catch me. *(She starts to chant)* Can't catch me-ee, can't catch me-ee …

Mary comes in. She is carrying a prayer book.

Mary Do you have to make so much noise? I was trying to pray.

Edward You're always praying.

Catherine Oh come now, Mary, don't be cross. It's Christmas after all. *(To Thomas)* Please ask the King when he would like to see the children.

Thomas But you still haven't told me …

Catherine We'll talk later.

Thomas bows and goes out.

Edward Auntie Catherine, you be Blind Man!

Catherine Later, Edward. Will you help me pick the presents up?

Edward I don't see why I should do that. I'm a prince and I'm going to be King. Princes don't pick things up.

Catherine If you help me pick them up, you can open the first one.

Edward Oh, all right then.

Catherine and Edward pick up the presents.

Mary *(whispering to Elizabeth)* Why should she tell us what to do?

Elizabeth I like Auntie Catherine.

Mary *(crossly)* She's not your aunt.

Elizabeth I think she's going to marry Daddy.

Mary Nonsense!

Elizabeth It's not nonsense. I heard him talking about it.

Mary You're making it up! Who was he talking to?

Elizabeth I'm not telling you.

Mary What did he say?

Elizabeth I'm not telling you.

Mary You didn't hear anything! I don't believe you.

Edward There! Done! I want to open a present. I want to open a present now!

Catherine All right. This one's from Mary.

Edward tears off the paper.

Edward *(sadly)* It's a prayer book. I want a ship. One like Daddy's ship, the *Mary Rose*, with sails and things! *(He starts to cry.)*

Catherine *(gently)* Edward, say "thank you" to Mary.

Edward No! *(To Mary)* When I'm King, I shall order you to give me good presents.

Mary Here we go again!

Edward Well, I shall be King. I'm Daddy's heir.

Elizabeth We know that, Edward, and it's not fair. Mary's older than you. So am I. You shouldn't be the heir. You're the heir, it's not fair. You're the heir, it's not fair. You're the …

Edward Stop it! I'm the heir because you're girls. Girls can't be King.

Elizabeth Girls can be Queens.

Edward Well, Mary isn't going to be Queen, and nor will you. I'm going to be King. Daddy says so. Mary won't be Queen unless something happens to me.

Mary Don't tempt me!

Edward Auntie Catherine! She's bullying me!

Catherine Mary!

Mary I'm sick and tired of it! Edward, Daddy's pet. Cry baby, Edward!

Edward *(to Mary)* At least Daddy loved my Mummy.

Catherine Edward …

Edward	*(still talking to Mary)* Daddy didn't love your Mummy. He sent her away.
Mary	Don't you dare say that!
Elizabeth	Leave Mary alone!
Edward	*(to Elizabeth)* And Daddy had your Mummy's head chopped off! *(He acts it out)* Swish! Thump!
Catherine	That will do! This is Christmas, the time of goodwill. Edward, don't tease Mary.
Edward	But I …
Catherine	Edward, tell Mary you're sorry.
Edward	Sorry.
Catherine	And Mary's sorry, too – aren't you, Mary?

Mary glares at Catherine.

Catherine	Mary – it is Christmas. A time for love.

Mary nods crossly.

Catherine	Good – then we're all friends again. Will Sommers is coming soon to make us all laugh.

Mary Oh, not Will Sommers. He's the worst jester in the world!

Elizabeth Auntie Catherine, he's rotten. And he's got bad breath, and he just shouts, "I say, I say, I say …"

Catherine We'll see, shall we? Now, whose turn is it to open a present?

Edward It's still mine! I want a good present – not a stupid prayer book!

Catherine Well, I have a present for you, Edward. I have some good news. Can you guess what it is?

Edward shakes his head.

Catherine Edward, you're going to be married.

Edward *(horrified)* Married? What … you mean … to a girl?

Elizabeth No, to a chicken! What do you think, silly?

Catherine Elizabeth, please! Edward, you are going to be betrothed to a princess.

Edward What does "beetrooted" mean?

Mary Betrothed. It means you've got to marry her.

Edward	But I don't want to get married to a soppy girl! Girls don't do anything interesting. They just dance and do sewing. Wait a moment! Did you say a princess?
Catherine	*(smiling)* That's right.
Edward	Oh well, that's different. I don't mind so much if she's a princess. What's her name?
Catherine	Mary.
Edward	Oh, no! Not another Mary.
Mary	*(crossly)* Mary's a very good name.
Edward	Hmmm. Is she beautiful?
Catherine	So people say. I haven't seen her myself.
Edward	Is she rich?
Catherine	Yes.
Edward	How old is she?
Catherine	I'm not sure. About three …
Edward	*(shocked)* Three years old?
Catherine	Three months old.

Elizabeth and Mary laugh.

Edward   What? I'm not marrying a baby! Babies dribble and blow bubbles and keep on being sick all over the place! I want to marry a beautiful princess, not change her nappies!

Catherine   You don't have to marry her now, you silly. You won't get married until you're King.

Edward   You're not to call me silly. I'm going to be King!

Edward sulks. Will Sommers, the King's jester, enters.

Will Sommers   I say, I say, I say!

Elizabeth   *(to Catherine)* I told you that's what he'd say!

Will Sommers Riddle me this! What is brown and sticky?

**Elizabeth
and Mary** *(bored)* A stick.

Will Sommers Oh – you've heard it. I know!
Knock knock.

Edward Come in.

Will Sommers No, no. You say "Who's there?"

Edward Why? We know it's you. We can see you.

Will Sommers It's a joke. You have to say "Who's there?"

Elizabeth Who's there?

Will Sommers Mary.

Nobody says anything.

Will Sommers You say "Mary who?"

Catherine Mary who?

**Elizabeth
and Mary** *(bored)* Mary Christmas.

Will Sommers Oh, you've heard that one as well.

Mary We've heard them all. You've been telling the same jokes since I was a little girl.

Thomas enters with more presents.

Thomas What are you doing here, Jester? We don't need you.

Catherine Thomas, that's not very kind.

Thomas Why should I be kind? He made up some stupid joke about my name last week – he said he wanted to "See more" of me. Very funny. Your jokes are as old as you are!

Will Sommers Well, here's a brand new joke for you. When will Catherine Parr not be Catherine Parr?

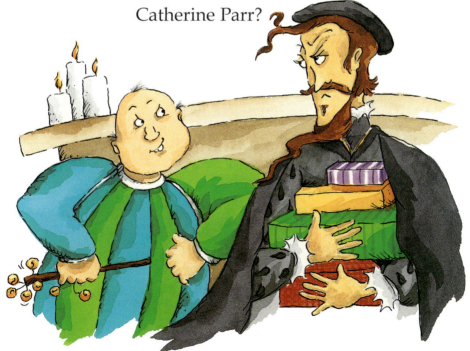

Elizabeth	I don't know.
Will Sommers	When she's Queen Catherine!
Thomas	*(slowly)* What do you mean, Jester?
Elizabeth	*(to Mary)* I told you! I told you! Daddy's going to marry Auntie Catherine!
Thomas	*(to Will)* Be gone!

Will Sommers exits.

Thomas	*(to Catherine)* Is this true? I must know. Is it true?
Catherine	It's true. I was going to tell you later. The King spoke to me yesterday. He asked me to marry him.

Elizabeth	Told you! Told you!
Thomas	But you're going to marry me! He knows that! I'll not have it. I'll go and tell him.
Catherine	And if you do, you'll have your head cut off. There's nothing we can do. I shall have to marry him.
Thomas	I see. You want to be Queen. I'll not stand in your way. *(He bows)* My lady.

Thomas exits.

Catherine	Thomas! That's not what I meant at all!
Edward	Are you going to be our Mummy?
Mary	I'm losing count of the mothers I've had.

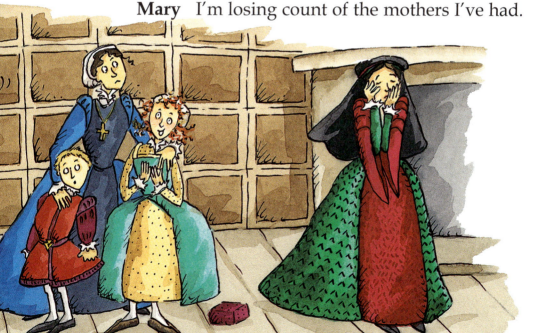

19

Catherine Children – it's not what I want. Do you understand? We all have to do what the King says.

Elizabeth Will you be a good mother?

Catherine Yes. I promise.

Elizabeth So that's our Christmas present – a new mother.

Edward I'd rather have a ship.

Mary Edward!

Edward But I suppose a new mother is better than nothing.

Elizabeth and Mary nod.

Catherine Thank you. Now let us go and find the King. Perhaps this year, we can have a real family Christmas.

They exit.

What happened next?

In 1543 King Henry VIII did marry Catherine Parr. She was his wife and nurse until he died in 1547.

Then Catherine Parr married Thomas Seymour, but she died a year later.

Edward became King Edward VI when his father died. He was nine years old. He died in 1553 at the age of 15.

After Edward died, Mary became Queen. She put Elizabeth in prison. Mary died in 1558.

Then Elizabeth became Queen Elizabeth I.

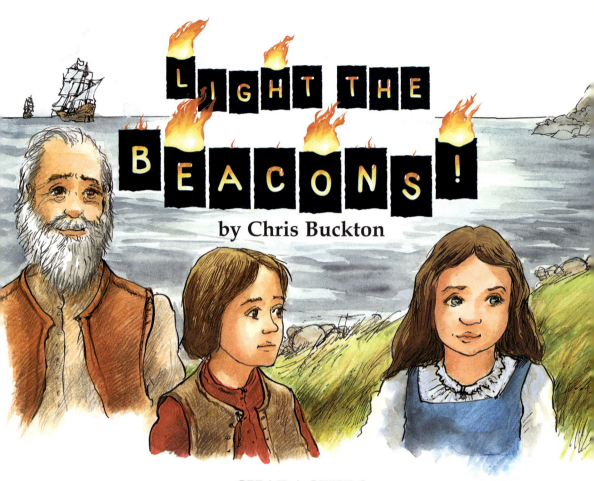

LIGHT THE BEACONS!

by Chris Buckton

CHARACTERS

Narrator
Matthew as an old man.
He is an old sailor thinking
about the past. He speaks
slowly and thoughtfully.

Bess Prior, aged 11
She is the eldest of the Prior
children. She's quiet and
sensible. She understands
Matthew's feelings.

Matthew Prior, aged 9
He has very strong feelings.
He wants to be a hero and
doesn't like being told what
to do.

Hal Prior, aged 6
He is excited about the war
and always curious about
everything. He has a pet dog
called Mop.

Thomas Prior

He is the children's father and village watchman. He is worried about the war. He is a very responsible person.

Anne Prior

She is the children's mother. She can be quite bossy but she's got a kind heart.

Sound effects

Door
Pots and pans
Wind whistling
Distant drums and shouting
Dog barking
Flint being struck (scraping sound)
Fire (crumpling paper)
Church bells (chime bar)

Time: July/August 1588

Setting: a village on the south coast of England near Plymouth

PROLOGUE

Narrator *(Matthew as an old man)*   When I was a lad I longed for adventure. I had dreams, just like all children since the world began.

Most of all, I dreamed of being a sailor and fighting for Admiral Drake. He was my hero.

Our family lived near Plymouth. The year that I was nine, we were all afraid that the Spanish Armada would attack us. The ships in Plymouth harbour were getting ready to defend England. I wanted to join the navy. Sometimes they would take on boys if they were tall enough …

24

Scene One

The Priors' cottage on 30 July, early morning. Anne, Thomas, Bess and Hal are at breakfast.

Thomas *(worried)* They say in the village that it can't be long now. We must pray and hope to be saved from our enemies.

Anne *(anxiously)* The preacher says that our enemies will torture us. I fear for our children. I fear for ourselves.

Hal *(not really scared, he thinks it's all a game)* What will they do to us? Will they put us in a dungeon?

Bess Our ships will defeat the Spanish! Drake set their ships afire last year!

Thomas But our ships are small. Our sailors may be brave but the Spanish outnumber us. Their galleons with their great sails will sweep us up like crumbs on their table.

Anne Let's have no more of that dangerous talk. Hal, go and call your brother for his breakfast. Is he going to lie in bed all day? There's work to be done.

Hal runs off. Bess looks guilty and starts to speak.

Bess Mother, I –

Hal *(shouting)* Matthew isn't here! His bed's empty!

He comes clattering back downstairs and sits at the table.

Bess Mother, don't be afraid. He's safe enough. I know where he is.

Anne Well, tell us girl, tell us at once.

Bess He's gone down to the harbour. He wants to join the navy.

Thomas *(laughing)* The boy's mad! He's only a child! They won't look at him!

Bess *(fiercely)* Don't laugh at him! Didn't you have dreams when you were a boy? He wants to help.

She is interrupted by the door opening. Matthew comes in, head hanging, looking miserable. He sits down at the table.

Hal *(excited)* Did they take you, Matt? *(Bess kicks him)* Ouch!

Anne *(gently)* Eat your porridge now, Matthew. You're just a boy. Be patient.

Matthew *(beginning to cry)* But the danger is here now! I want to help. I want to fight.

A tear drops into his porridge.

Thomas If you want to help, then come up the hillside and stack logs with me. I must be ready to light the beacon as soon as the Armada is sighted. The fire will be a signal to our soldiers. They will defend us if the Spanish land on our shores.

Matthew *(scornfully)* Lighting the beacon isn't real war.

Hal *(excited)* It is, it is! Father is watchman, he'll send the signal! Can I help too?

Thomas I would be glad of you all today.

Anne *(worried)* You're not well, Thomas, you're shivering. You have a fever coming. Can you not ask neighbour William to take your watch?

Thomas *(firmly)* No, I must do my duty. I must keep the watch.

Scene Two

The hillside that afternoon. Wind blowing, larks singing. Matthew, Bess, Hal and their father are stacking wood at the top of the hill. There is a big iron fire basket on a post. Next to it is a little wooden hut. Thomas is coughing.

Thomas	As soon as they see the Spanish ships, they'll light the beacon on the Plymouth hill. And that fire will be the signal for me to light this beacon.
Bess	And then the next village will see it and light theirs …
Hal	And then the next …
Matthew	And the next, all the way to London and the Queen!
Thomas	That's right. The chain mustn't be broken.
Bess	So the whole of England will know that the Armada is come. And the soldiers will come to defend us.
Hal	But how will you light the fire quickly enough?
Thomas	See here, I keep some dry tinder in this pocket. And my flint in its little box. I've laid the wood all ready in the iron basket. I'll need a steady hand.
Hal	What if it rains?
Thomas	Here's my hut for shelter. And I have some dry logs inside.

Hal It doesn't have a seat for you to rest on. You'll get tired.

Thomas There's no seat in case I should fall asleep. I must watch every moment.

They look down towards Plymouth.

Bess I can see the harbour … and there's the Plymouth beacon ready to be lit.

Hal What if the Spanish land in Plymouth? Are the soldiers ready?

Matthew Drake wants to fight the Spanish at sea, and stop them from landing. That's right, Father, isn't it?

Thomas Yes, son. The army will do their best, but they're not strong. They're not well trained. Better to fight the battles at sea.

Matthew And we have better sailors than the Spanish.

Bess And Drake can do anything. He raided the ships in Cadiz harbour and singed the King of Spain's beard!

Hal But, Father, you said the English ships are small, next to the great Spanish galleons.

Thomas Maybe small ships will be faster. *(Wearily, coughing, shivering)* We must trust in God.

Bess *(anxiously)* You're not well, Father … and it's a lonely job.

Thomas I must watch. And you must help your mother while I'm away up here on the hillside. Go back now. And bring me my supper tonight.

The children run off down the hillside, waving and calling goodbye as they go.

Scene Three

The hillside on the same night. Strong wind blowing. The children are scrambling through the bracken, climbing the hill breathlessly. They are carrying their father's supper in a basket covered with a cloth.

Hal   Do you think Father's afraid, up here alone in the dark?

Matthew   *(scornfully)* I wouldn't be afraid.

Bess   He'll be glad of warm broth and bread.

They reach the top – but there's no sign of Thomas.

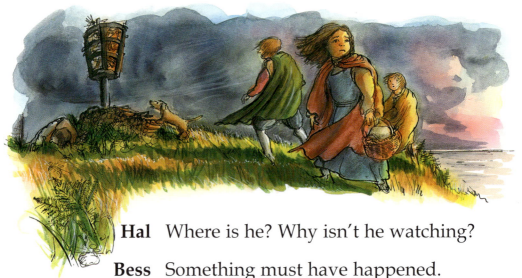

Hal   Where is he? Why isn't he watching?

Bess   Something must have happened.

Matthew   Look! Over there! Father is lying by the wood pile!

Bess   He's sick. Sick with fever. We must cover him with our cloaks. We must keep him warm.

The children take their cloaks off and tuck them round their father.

Bess   Can you hear me, Father? We're here, we'll get help.

Thomas   *(weakly)* Watch hard for smoke … Look towards Plymouth … Keep your eyes …

Hal   *(crying)* Father! Wake up! I'm frightened. We must get help.

Matthew   *(urgently)* But we must keep watch as well. The chain mustn't be broken!

Bess   Hal, could you be brave enough to run back to the cottage and raise the alarm? Matthew and I must stay on watch.

Hal   Do you know how to light the tinder?

Matthew   I know how to strike the flint.

Bess   Let's pray that help will come before we need to.

Hal   I'll go like the wind.

Matthew   Then run, Hal!

Hal runs off.

Matthew Keep your eyes fixed on Plymouth. I'll find Father's tinder and flint.

He searches Thomas' pockets and finds them. Thomas groans but doesn't speak.

Matthew Father is burning hot. What if he should …

Bess *(briskly)* We mustn't think about it. Hal will get help. We must just watch.

Bess and Matthew keep their eyes fixed on Plymouth.

Matthew *(teeth chattering)* Can you see the harbour lights? My eyes are aching from staring into the darkness.

Bess Let's sing to keep our spirits up.

She starts to hum a tune.

Matthew *(quietly)* I said I wouldn't be afraid but it's so dark. I'm glad you're here too, Bess.

Bess *(excited)* Look, Matthew – what's that? Is it smoke rising up? Is it? Can it be?

Sounds of drums and shouting in the distance.

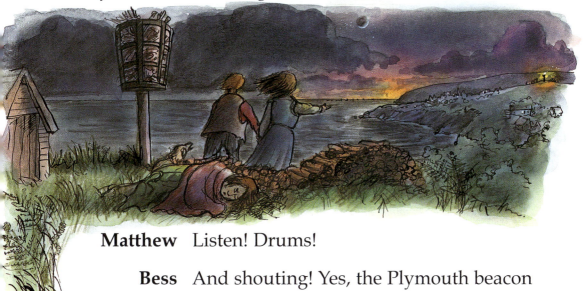

Matthew Listen! Drums!

Bess And shouting! Yes, the Plymouth beacon
is blazing!

Matthew The Armada is come! *(Shivering)* Oh Bess,
I'm afraid to do this alone. What if I can't
light the beacon? What if we fail?

Bess Think how we strike the flint for the fire
at home. We won't fail.

Matthew I can feel my heart like a hammer.

Bess My hand is shaking. But we won't fail.

Sounds of flint being struck.

Bess Look! A spark is catching! Put on more
tinder!

Rustling sounds. Then a pause.

Matthew   (*desperately*) Oh no! The spark's gone out!

Bess   (*urgently*) Try again! Quick, we only have a little tinder left.

Sound of flint again. The children hold their breath.

Bess   (*whispering*) There's a spark!

Matthew   The wind is too strong. I'll shield the fire with my jerkin.

He takes off his jerkin and holds it in front of the fire.

Matthew   (*hopefully*) The spark is still alight! It's glowing … and growing!

Sound of fire burning.

Bess I can hear it crackling!

Matthew *(excited)* It's alight! We've done it! Quick, Bess, more wood!

Bess The smoke is streaming in the wind. We've done it!

The children cheer and whoop in excitement.

Thomas *(stirring, muttering)* Don't break the chain!

Scene Four

The Priors' cottage the following day. Thomas is safely in bed. The children are clustered round. Anne comes in carrying a hot drink.

Anne *(scolding)* Now lie still, Thomas, and drink this hot posset. I've picked herbs from the garden to make you well again.

Thomas *(weakly)* How good it is to be safe at home. Last night was like a dark dream. I just remember the world seeming to turn round …

Hal You had fainted, Father. We found you lying on the ground.

Bess And Hal here was so brave, he ran back alone and fetched neighbour William. William carried you on his back.

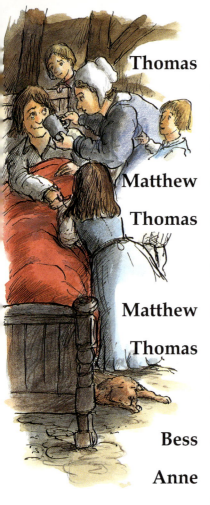

Thomas   *(proudly)* You were all brave. Bess, you were as brave as Good Queen Bess herself. And Hal, like her father King Henry. *(He stops to cough)*

Matthew   *(eagerly)* What about me, Father?

Thomas   *(laughing)* I said you were nothing but a child, and you said that lighting the beacon wasn't real war.

Matthew   I know better now.

Thomas   Aye, and so do I. You did a man's job. Drake himself would be proud to have you as a son.

Bess   *(proudly)* The chain wasn't broken.

Anne   They say in the market that the beacons burned all night. The fires blazed all along the south coast.

Matthew   Father, our ships sailed out of the harbour. They're lying in wait, and the wind has driven the Armada up the channel.

Thomas   We'll pluck their feathers little by little. But it won't be done for many a year. One day, my boy, maybe one day you'll be at Drake's side …

EPILOGUE

Sounds of church bells pealing.

Narrator I'll never forget the church bells and the cheering when the Armada was defeated, and their ships driven north by the storms. All those great galleons wrecked on the rocks.

And one thing I keep by me always.

Gets a medal out of his pocket, holds it lovingly.

A medal to remind us of that victory. I know its words by heart: "God blew and they were scattered".

It wasn't the end of the war, though. My father was right. When I was fourteen I joined the navy and sailed with Drake against the Spanish.

But that night was the start of it all – the night I lit the beacon. That was the beginning of the real war for me.

Church bells sound again.

TIMELINE

April 1587 Admiral Drake "singes the King of Spain's beard" in Cadiz.

May 1588 Armada sails from Lisbon.

22 July English fleet anchors in Plymouth.

30 July Sea captain tells Drake that the Armada is sighted in Plymouth Sound.

30 July Beacons lit.

31 July Wind drives Spanish up the Channel with the English behind them. Battle near Plymouth.

1–2 August Battle near Portland Bill.

3–4 August Battle near Isle of Wight.

7 August Spanish anchor at Calais. English send fireships into Calais harbour.

8 August Battle of Gravelines.

21 August Spanish ships driven north by storms.

26 October Last ship of Armada sinks off Irish coast.

1596 Death of Drake.

1603 Death of Queen Elizabeth I.

Yellow Stockings

by Julia Donaldson

Introduction

The Globe Theatre was in Southwark, across the River Thames from London Town. William Shakespeare wrote many of the plays performed there, and acted in them as well. *Twelfth Night* was probably written in 1601, towards the end of Queen Elizabeth's reign.

In the 1990s the Globe Theatre was rebuilt. It reopened in 1997.

Pip Fleet
A boy actor, aged 13

Annie Fleet
His twin sister, a seamstress

Mistress Fleet
Their mother, a tailor

An apothecary
A man who prepares and sells medicines.

Sir Perry
A gentleman who is very concerned about his clothes and appearance, a "fop"

A fruit-seller

Scene One *A London street.*

Fruit-seller Fine apples, apples fine!
A farthing for four, a ha-penny for nine.

Enter Pip.

Pip I'll have nine. But let me taste one first.

Fruit-seller (*suspiciously*) Let's see your ha-penny then.

Pip Why? Don't you trust me?

Fruit-seller I never trust a schoolboy.

Pip I'm not a schoolboy. I'm an actor. You sell your apples at the Globe Theatre, don't you? Didn't you see me in the play last week? I was the girl who drowned herself.

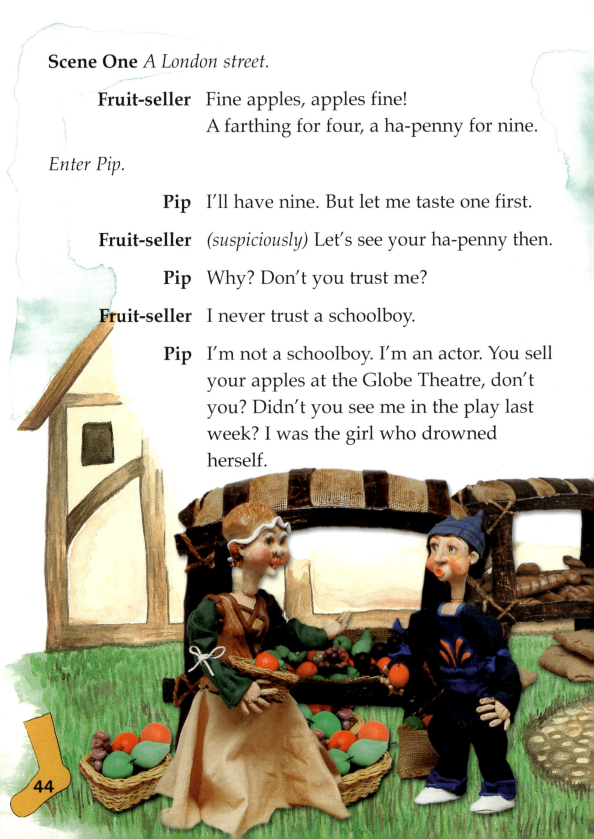

44

Fruit-seller   So you were, and I nearly drowned too –
in my own tears! Go on then, taste an
apple, but don't make me cry like that
again.

Pip   I won't. The next play's a comedy. It's
called *Twelfth Night*. I'm going to be the
main character. She's called Viola.

Fruit-seller   Do you always act as a girl?

Pip   Usually. It makes my sister furious. She'd
love to be on the stage herself.
She doesn't think it's fair that girls aren't
allowed to.

Fruit-seller   I hope you don't drown yourself in
this play.

Pip No. I do get shipwrecked, but I end up on an island.

Fruit-seller You're a good swimmer then?

Pip Viola is. I'm not. To tell the truth, I can't swim!

Fruit-seller You're good at eating apples, though.

Pip Yes. That was very tasty.

Fruit-seller Do you still want nine?

Pip Well, there's just one problem. I don't have a ha-penny.

Fruit-seller I knew it all along! Be off with you!

Pip I'll see you at the Globe! And thanks for the apple! *(He runs off.)*

Scene Two *A tailor's shop.*

Enter Mistress Fleet.

Ms Fleet Annie! Annie!

Enter Annie, knitting a pair of bright yellow stockings.

Annie What is it, Mother?

Ms Fleet Haven't you finished those stockings for the play yet?

Annie I nearly have. What a horrible yellow!

46

No one in their right mind would want
to wear them.

Ms Fleet Well, speed up. You know Pip's promised
to take all the costumes across to the
Globe in the boat this afternoon. *(There is
the ting of the shop bell.)* Maybe this is him
now. Oh no! It's Sir Perry.

Sir Perry Good morning, Mistress
Fleet. Is my doublet
ready?

Ms Fleet Yes, Sir Perry. Here it is.

Sir Perry Very good, very good –
but I'm not so sure now
about the sleeves. I
fancy those turned-back

cuffs are going out of fashion. Several of the gentlemen at court are wearing wrist ruffs. Pray make me a pair of wrist ruffs, Mistress Fleet.

Ms Fleet Very well, Sir Perry. What colour?

Sir Perry Let me think ... yellow. A bright yellow, a dazzling yellow, a yellow like ... like that pair of stockings your girl is knitting! In fact, I'll take the stockings too. They should turn a few heads at court.

Ms Fleet I'm sorry, Sir, but those stockings are for one of the actors in Mr Shakespeare's new play.

Sir Perry Then knit me another pair just the same. And make sure they're ready in time for the play.

Ms Fleet Are you going to see it, then?

Sir Perry Of course! I never miss a new play. I caused quite a stir at the last one in my crimson satin cloak. I fancy more eyes were on me than on the actors! Good morning, Mistress Fleet. *(He exits.)*

Annie Oh no! Not another pair of yellow stockings! I can't bear it!

Ms Fleet   Stop moaning, Annie – it's all good business. Now, mind the shop while I go and buy some more yellow silk.

She exits and Pip enters.

Pip   *(quoting from the play)* "What country, friends, is this?"

Annie   *(scornfully)* Brilliant, you've learnt your first line!

Pip   Wrong reply – you're suppose to say "It is Illyria, Lady."

Annie   I wish it really was Illyria. Then I could be having impossible adventures instead of knitting awful stockings.

Pip   What do you mean, impossible adventures? Are you criticising Mr Shakespeare's play?

Annie   Well, it's all a bit unlikely, isn't it? Viola getting shipwrecked and then disguising herself as a man and fooling everyone! You're not telling me that could happen in real life?

Pip   I don't see why not.

Annie   And then her twin brother turning up on the same island and everyone mixing them up.

Pip   What's wrong with that?

Annie   Oh, come on, Pip! We're twins but no one ever thinks I'm you.

Pip   Maybe if you wore my clothes they would.

Annie   I don't think so, somehow.

Pip   You're just in a bad mood. Why don't you test me on my lines? Let's do the scene where Viola meets Lady Olivia.

He hands Annie his lines.

Annie All right then. I know, I'll wear Lady Olivia's veil! Here it is. *(She picks up a veil from the top of a pile of costumes and covers her face with it.)* Well, go on, say your first line.

Pip *(acting Viola)* "The honourable ... the honourable ..."

Annie *(prompting him)* "The honourable lady of the house, which is she?"

Pip Hey! I'm supposed to say that.

Annie I know; I was just prompting you. Honestly, Pip, I think I know these lines better than you do!

Enter Mistress Fleet.

Ms Fleet Annie, stop prancing around with that veil. You know it's for the play.

Annie I'm just testing Pip on his lines.

Ms Fleet Haven't you learnt them yet, Pip? You're leaving it a bit late in the day.

Pip Well, what about your costumes? They don't seem to be ready. Annie's still knitting those yellow stockings.

Annie It's your fault for making me test you on your lines. Anyway, I'm on the last row. I'll have finished by the time you've loaded the other clothes into the boat.

Ms Fleet Can you manage them all, Pip?

Pip I'll have to, won't I?

He glares at Annie, who is still knitting, and picks up an armful of clothes. As they exit, the apothecary enters, carrying a tray of medicines.

Apothecary Business is busy, I see.

Ms Fleet Yes. We've been making costumes for the new play at the Globe Theatre. My son is acting in it, too.

Apothecary I'm sorry to hear that. The playhouse is the haunt of the devil.

Ms Fleet What can I do for you, Sir?

Apothecary The strap from my tray of medicines has snapped. Can you make me a new one?

Ms Fleet Certainly, Sir. What colour would you like?

Apothecary Something plain and dark.

Ms Fleet How about this brown braid? If you empty your tray I can fix it for you while you wait.

Apothecary Thank you. You seem to be a sensible lady in spite of your unfortunate connection with the theatre.

Ms Fleet Is it just medicines you sell? No sweets or face powder?

Apothecary Certainly not. Those are the wares of the devil.

Enter Annie, in a panic.

Annie Mother, Mother! Something terrible has happened! Pip started rowing before I'd finished the stockings.

53

Ms Fleet That's not so terrible.

Annie No, but then I finished them and threw them to him, and he lost his balance and fell into the river!

Apothecary Heaven preserve him!

Ms Fleet Quick! Can you swim, Sir?

Apothecary Er ...

Annie It's all right. He's been rescued by a young woman, a fruit-seller. She jumped in and saved him.

Ms Fleet Thank goodness for that!

Annie Here they come now.

Enter Pip and the fruit-seller, both wet. Pip is sneezing.

Ms Fleet Oh, Pip! Oh, thank you, young lady, thank you! Oh, you're both soaking! Annie, fetch some towels!

Apothecary I have some lily root here, Mistress Fleet. If you boil it in white wine it is a cure for the shivering fits.

Fruit-seller I think some dry clothes might be a better cure.

Ms Fleet Let's all go into the back room. The fire is lit in there. Annie, bring some clothes through.

Annie Yes, Mother. And then I'll row the costumes across.

They all go into the back room. Annie takes in some clothes and the apothecary takes in his tray.

Apothecary *(as he goes out)* It is a warning from Heaven. The boy should leave the theatre!

Scene Three *Pip's bedroom, a few days later.*

Enter Mistress Fleet, Annie and the apothecary.

Ms Fleet The apothecary has come to see you again, Pip.

Apothecary Let me feel your brow. Hmmm, there is still some fever.

Annie It's not the plague, is it, Sir? Please say it's not the plague.

Apothecary No, there are no swellings. God willing, the boy has been spared. Keep giving him the boiled lily root, and some of this onion and vinegar drink. That should bring the fever down. And above all, keep him away from the theatre!

Pip   (*whispering*) Will the drink bring my voice back?

Apothecary   Yes, in a week or so. Some oil and gunpowder mixture might bring it back even sooner.

Pip   How soon?

Apothecary   A couple of days perhaps.

Pip   But the play starts this afternoon!

Ms Fleet   That's too bad, Pip. They'll just have to find someone else to play Viola.

Apothecary   In my opinion, they would do better to close down the theatre.

Ms Fleet   Thank you for all your help, Sir. I'll see you out.

Exit Ms Fleet and the apothecary.

Pip *(still whispering)* I must go to the theatre! I'll be thrown out of the play if I don't. I'm already in trouble for being late learning my lines.

Annie Pip ... I know your lines. I've tested you on them often enough.

Pip Stop boasting, Annie.

Annie I'm not boasting. I've got an idea. You know you said people might think I was you if I wore your clothes? Well, why don't I give it a try?

Pip What, you act Viola? You must be joking.

Annie No, I'm not. Leave it to me, Pip.

Scene Four *The Globe Theatre.*

The first performance of Twelfth Night *is just ending. The fruit-seller and Sir Perry are among the audience.*

Annie *(singing on the stage)*
A great while ago the world begun,
With hey ho, the wind and the rain,
But that's all one, our play is done,
And we'll strive to please you every day.

Everyone claps. She bows and exits.

Fruit-seller Did you enjoy the play, Sir Perry?

Sir Perry To tell the truth, I preferred the last one.

Fruit-seller Viola was good, though, wasn't she? He, I mean.

Sir Perry Ah yes, young Pip Fleet.

Fruit-seller You could have sworn she was a real woman – even though she was pretending to be a man for most of the play.

Sir Perry I know the Fleet family well. They made my doublet. I expect you've been admiring the wrist ruffs?

Fruit-seller Sorry, Sir Perry, I was too busy watching the play. Wasn't that idiot in those awful yellow stockings funny?

Sir Perry Not particularly.

Fruit-seller The way he was strutting around – he really thought Lady Olivia fancied him. Yellow stockings! I nearly died laughing!

Sir Perry I can't say I saw the joke.

Enter Ms Fleet.

Fruit-seller Good afternoon, Mistress Fleet. You must be proud of Pip.

Ms Fleet Yes, I am.

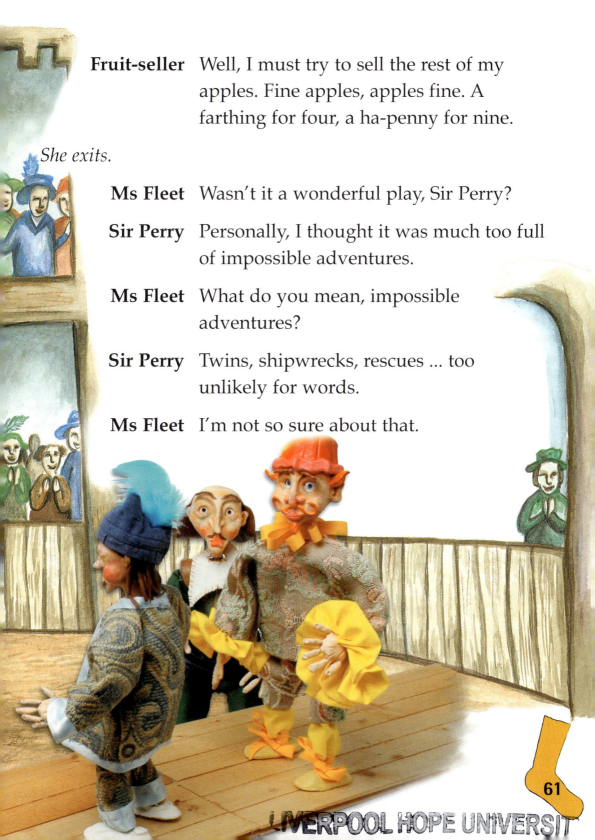

Fruit-seller   Well, I must try to sell the rest of my apples. Fine apples, apples fine. A farthing for four, a ha-penny for nine.

She exits.

Ms Fleet   Wasn't it a wonderful play, Sir Perry?

Sir Perry   Personally, I thought it was much too full of impossible adventures.

Ms Fleet   What do you mean, impossible adventures?

Sir Perry   Twins, shipwrecks, rescues ... too unlikely for words.

Ms Fleet   I'm not so sure about that.

61

Sir Perry   And then, in real life, no one would mistake a woman for a man like that, would they? I certainly wouldn't.

Ms Fleet   If you say so, Sir Perry.

Sir Perry   By the bye, did your daughter come to the play, Mistress Fleet? I would like a word with her.

Ms Fleet   Er ... no, she was too busy sewing.

Sir Perry   A pity. A pity.

Ms Fleet   Can I give her a message?

Sir Perry   Yes. I would like another pair of stockings.

Ms Fleet   *(trying not to laugh)* Very well. Yellow ones again, Sir Perry?

Sir Perry   No. Strangely enough, these yellow stockings are no longer to my liking. Pray ask your daughter to knit me some violet stockings.

Liverpool Hope University

This item is to be returned on or before the last due date stamped below .

Items can be renewed 3 times unseen.If a fourth renewal is required the item must be brought to the library.